FRESH AIR
GROUP EXPERIENCE
PARTICIPANT'S GUIDE

FRESH AIR

A GROUP EXPERIENCE PARTICIPANT'S GUIDE

*trading stale spiritual obligation for a life-altering,
energizing, experience-it-everyday relationship with God*

BASED ON THE BOOK BY

CHRIS HODGES

TYNDALE
MOMENTUM™

The nonfiction imprint of
Tyndale House Publishers, Inc.

Visit Tyndale online at www.tyndale.com.

Visit Tyndale Momentum online at www.tyndalemomentum.com.

Go to www.churchofthehighlands.com to learn more about Church of the Highlands and Chris Hodges.

TYNDALE, Tyndale Momentum, and Tyndale's quill logo are registered trademarks of Tyndale House Publishers, Inc. The Tyndale Momentum logo is a trademark of Tyndale House Publishers, Inc. Tyndale Momentum is the nonfiction imprint of Tyndale House Publishers, Inc., Carol Stream, Illinois.

Fresh Air Group Experience Participant's Guide: Trading Stale Spiritual Obligation for a Life-Altering, Energizing, Experience-It-Everyday Relationship with God

Designed by Barry Smith and Dean H. Renninger

Published in association with the literary agency of Winters and King, Inc., 2448 E. 81st St., CityPlex Towers, Suite 5900, Tulsa, OK 74137.

For information about special discounts for bulk purchases, please contact Tyndale House Publishers at csresponse@tyndale.com or call 800-323-9400.

ISBN 978-1-4143-8682-9 Softcover

Printed in the United States of America

23	22	21	20	19	18
9	8	7	6	5	4

CONTENTS

ABOUT THE FRESH AIR
GROUP EXPERIENCE DVD

The guide you're holding is the companion to the *Fresh Air Group Experience DVD*: a simple, eight- to ten-week curriculum designed to move participants into a vibrant, passionate relationship with God. Inspired by the book *Fresh Air*, written by Pastor Chris Hodges, the study was developed with the aim of providing accessibility and approachability for people with an array of schedules and lifestyles. From DVD messages and icebreaker ideas to leader tips and simple self-assessment questions, every element of this study was created to take you on an adventure with the Lord that is challenging, encouraging, and enjoyable.

Whether you are looking for ways to deepen your Christian walk or are just beginning to discover what the faith journey is about, *Fresh Air* can help you apply some life-giving principles from the Scriptures and introduce you to your best friend and advocate, the Holy Spirit. The Lord always meant for us to have a helper in this life, because let's face it, we need one! Together, we'll pull back the curtains of myth and tradition and learn what the Bible says about the one whom the Father sent to be our Counselor.

ABOUT CHRIS HODGES

Chris Hodges is founding and senior pastor of Church of the Highlands, with campuses all across the state of Alabama. Since it began in 2001, Church of the Highlands has experienced tremendous growth and is known for its life-giving culture and focus on leading people to an intimate relationship with God.

Pastor Chris has a deep passion for developing leaders and planting life-giving churches. He cofounded ARC (Association of Related Churches) in 2001, which has launched hundreds of churches all across America. He also founded a coaching network called GROW, which trains and resources pastors to help them break barriers and reach their growth potential. Chris is also the founder and president of Highlands College, a ministry training school that trains and launches students into full-time ministry careers. Chris and his wife, Tammy, have five children and live in Birmingham, Alabama, where Church of the Highlands began. He speaks at conferences worldwide and is the author of *Fresh Air*.

HOW TO USE THIS
PARTICIPANT'S GUIDE

....

True to the title it bears, we've kept *Fresh Air* simple.
Each session in *Fresh Air* features a DVD message from
Pastor Chris that you'll watch at the beginning of small
group meetings, and inside the study guide you will find
a "Big Idea" summary, a recap of the previous week's
teaching, and discussion and study questions that pro-
mote interaction. Finally, for those who are leading
a group, we've included a Leader's Focus DVD message to help you prepare for the weekly meeting. We've
also ended this guide with ideas specifically for group
leaders.

Your group may choose to complete this study in either
eight or ten weeks. If you are part of an eight-session
group, you can complete the introduction and session 1
in your first week together. During your final meeting,
you can cover session 8 and the conclusion. If your group
is scheduled to meet for ten weeks, you can focus on the
introduction and conclusion during your opening and clos-
ing sessions, while spending additional time getting better
acquainted with the others in your group.

WHAT YOU'LL NEED

You will need the *Fresh Air Group Experience DVD* to watch together during each session. For the most complete group experience, each member is also encouraged to bring the following:

- His or her own copy of this participant's guide in which to follow along and take notes
- The book *Fresh Air* on which this study is based
- A Bible

OVERVIEW OF PARTICIPANT'S GUIDE ELEMENTS

RECAP

This is a short review of the previous week's message. It's also a great place to invite members to share their insights and experiences as they apply the teachings.

JUST FOR FUN

Here's a question to get your group talking.

BIG IDEA

This is a single idea for each session that sums up the main point or key idea of the week.

VIEW

This section allows you to reflect on Pastor Chris's weekly DVD teaching.

CATCH YOUR BREATH/LEARNING TO BREATHE

Here you can respond to engaging questions designed to encourage discussion and group interaction while moving people closer to God and others.

PRAY

Each week you'll find a suggested fresh air prayer focus.

NOTES

Use this space to jot down notes and insights during your small-group session.

GOING DEEPER

Each session in the participant's guide ends with a corresponding section of teaching notes called "Going Deeper." These are a supplement to the DVD and discussion questions, and may be particularly helpful to leaders as they prepare for each week's meeting.

SUGGESTED SCHEDULE FOR SMALL GROUP MEETINGS

1. Fellowship
2. Welcome and recap (10 minutes)
3. Watch the DVD (15 minutes)
4. Discuss (35 minutes)
5. Pray (10 minutes)
6. Dismiss on time

RECOMMENDED READING

As you reflect on the material in each session, read the corresponding chapters from the book *Fresh Air*, which contain more insights from Pastor Chris Hodges on how to reinvigorate your relationship with God. Check the table of contents in this guide for a breakdown of how the sessions in the *Group Experience* guide correspond with the chapters in *Fresh Air*.

KEYS TO EXCELLENT SMALL GROUPS

....

Below you'll find some ways to make the most of your *Fresh Air* small group.

VALUING ONE ANOTHER

Be gentle and gracious to people with different levels of spiritual maturity, personal opinions, temperaments, or imperfections. We are all growing and in different places on the journey.

Create a safe place where people can be heard and feel loved. Please offer no quick answers, snap judgments, or simple fixes. Every member has something to contribute. Consider inviting participants to share a team role (like greeting, hosting, or teaching) or responsibility (like facilitating refreshments or prayer requests, or sharing a personal story or testimony).

LAUGHTER

Have fun! Don't take yourself too seriously. Create opportunities for humor, laugh at yourself, and relax. Laughter is great medicine for the soul. It's okay to share a funny story that has zero to do with the session. Everyone loves a good story; just keep it short!

CONFIDENTIALITY

Create an atmosphere of trust and safety by keeping anything that is shared in the group strictly confidential. People need a safe place to be open and honest. A healthy small group encourages sincerity and transparency, and every group member has a responsibility to uphold this standard by respecting privacy, so ask all members to commit to keeping group discussions in confidence.

TIME MANAGEMENT

If you are facilitating a group, keep track of the time. Have a predetermined stopping point when people have permission to leave. Members, simply call or e-mail your leader if you are going to be absent. Leaders, create a group calendar that lets everyone know ahead of time if there is a week you will not be meeting due to holidays, vacations, etc. Make every effort to arrive on time and leave on time. It is disruptive to the group when people arrive late each week, and it is inconsiderate when members linger in a host's home too late.

RELATIONSHIPS

Jesus did everything in relationship. Meaningful, encouraging relationships are foundational. Teaching, discussion, and prayer are all important parts of the group, but nothing surpasses the value of truly caring for one another. Use your God-given abilities to serve and love one another and to meet one another's needs. When you do this, the relationships will develop naturally.

GETTING STARTED

*There are far, far better things ahead
than any we leave behind.*

C. S. LEWIS

JUST FOR FUN

What is the best thing that has happened to you in the last week?

BIG IDEA

Fresh air changes your point of view. With it, you can make the switch from duty to devotion and live a life that's fulfilling, interesting, fun, and purposeful. Real life change happens in the context of relationship—first with God and then with people.

VIEW

. . . .

Watch the DVD session by Pastor Chris Hodges entitled "Getting Started." Look for answers to the following questions:

What are the three benefits of being in a small group?

What is the key idea that inspired this study?

LEARNING TO BREATHE

. . . .

1. *What is your opinion of church? Why?*

2. *How can your relationship with God be like a breath of fresh air?*

3. *What do you hope to gain through this small group?*

PRAY

Pray for group members to grow in their relationships with God and with others.

NOTES

THE DOLDRUMS

BASED ON CHAPTER 1 OF *FRESH AIR*

*Life is a storm, my young friend. You will bask
in the sunlight one moment, be shattered on
the rocks the next. What makes you a man is
what you do when that storm comes.*

ALEXANDRE DUMAS
The Count of Monte Cristo

RECAP

If you want to see significant change in your life, it starts
on the inside and is directly related to your commitment to
God as well as others. Healthy relationships can help you
grow and enjoy life in many wonderful ways.

JUST FOR FUN

Is there a person or movie that can always make you laugh?
Explain.

BIG IDEA

There is a gravitational pull for all of us toward the doldrums—the place where there's no wind, where we feel stifled and exhausted. We can move out of this place by being transparent and honest about our struggles. James 5:16 says, "Confess your sins to each other and pray for each other so that you may be healed."

VIEW

Watch the DVD session by Pastor Chris Hodges entitled "The Doldrums." Think about the following:

Have you ever experienced a season of being stuck in the doldrums?

What things helped you move out of the doldrums?

CATCH YOUR BREATH

Do any of these symptoms of dissatisfaction seem familiar?

- You feel like you're on a treadmill with no hope of escaping or moving forward.
- Life wears you out, and no amount of sleep relieves the weariness.

- What you hoped would bring you joy doesn't cut it anymore.
- You feel trapped in the life you've chosen.
- It seems the sum of your choices in life defines who you are.

LEARNING TO BREATHE

1. *What keeps you from being honest with others in relationships?*

2. *If you are in the doldrums now—or have been there in the past—consider what pushed you there: (1) you drifted away from God; (2) you were caught in one of life's disturbances; or (3) you felt weary and spiritually fatigued. Review pages 9 through 12 of* Fresh Air *as you consider your response.*

PRAY

Pray for group members to have the courage to talk to the Lord about the areas in life where they are stuck, and for them to take one step this week toward growth and confidence.

NOTES

GOING DEEPER

When we long for life without difficulty, remind
us that oaks grow strong under contrary winds
and diamonds are made under pressure.

PETER MARSHALL

Ever been in the doldrums? It's the place where you are only going through the motions. You simply exist: soul-weary and burned out, you bury your emotions just to survive the day.

Unfortunately, many believers have drifted to this place. Oh, we're not abandoning God or leaving the church, but neither are we fully alive or enjoying the abundant life Jesus said he came to bring. We're in this middle zone—this lifeless zone. We have gotten off course and now there is no wind to sustain us.

We end up in the doldrums when our lives revolve around *doing* rather than *being*. That's because real life flows more internally than externally. When we forget that and end up in the doldrums, it's time for a shift in focus. Are we driven by *internal* motivation or *external* motivation? (For example, there's a difference between obeying traffic laws out of fear of fines and jail time and obeying them to keep everyone safe from harm.)

If you're going to make it out of the doldrums, you

must make a shift on the inside, not the outside. The Good News that Jesus brought is about a transformation of the inner person that makes us different at our core.

So who are you at the center? Why do you do what you do? What do you want to do with your life? Where do you want to go? What dream has God placed in your heart that you've thought you could never pursue?

Let's discover how to put fresh air back into our sails.

To find out more about getting out of the doldrums, read chapter 1 in the book *Fresh Air*.

1. *The doldrums cause us to be in a state of doing rather than being. How have you chosen to try harder, work longer, or strived to change instead of depending on God?*

2. *When we are in a difficult season of life, it is easy to believe the lies of the enemy. How can we protect ourselves from believing those lies?*

3. *The Scriptures say that those who put their hope in God will never be disappointed (Isaiah 28:16; Romans 10:11). What do you have to gain by choosing to embrace God today?*

4. *In what area or situation of life have you given up hope, and how would your life be different if fresh air poured into that place?*

CHOOSE LIFE

BASED ON CHAPTERS 2 AND 3 OF *FRESH AIR*

And in the end, it's not the years in your life that count.
It's the life in your years.

ATTRIBUTED TO ABRAHAM LINCOLN

RECAP

When we find ourselves in a place that feels stagnant and lifeless, we need to find fresh air to propel us forward. Don't give up! As you will see, it's easier to fill your sails with wind than you may think.

JUST FOR FUN

If you could spend an entire day in one location and you had unlimited funds, where would it be?

BIG IDEA

Knowing and loving God is the key to our ultimate fulfillment in life.

VIEW

Watch the DVD session by Pastor Chris Hodges entitled "Choose Life."

What are fresh-air-culture qualities?

What is the difference between relationship and religion?

CATCH YOUR BREATH

A life-giving outlook breathes fresh air into any situation.

- Do you enjoy your relationship with God, participating out of delight rather than duty?
- Do you embrace your uniqueness and the calling that God has on your life?
- Do you feel empowered to be creative and pursue your dreams?

- Do you have a sense of purpose and focus, and live out this purpose every day?
- Do you laugh and find humor in all areas of life?
- Do you develop life-giving relationships by addressing hurts, wounds, and disappointments as they occur?
- Do you focus on others more than yourself?

LEARNING TO BREATHE

1. *When did you most recently notice a person or place that brought you fresh air? What were the circumstances? How did this person or location refresh you?*

2. *Are you in love with God? How can you tell?*

3. *Read Ephesians 3:17-19. How has God demonstrated his love to you in a tangible way? How have you shown God your love?*

4. *Review the seven qualities that Pastor Chris says produce spiritual health on pages 25 through 31 of* Fresh Air. *Which would you most like to develop? Why?*

PRAY

Pray for group members to develop genuine love and affection for God.

NOTES

GOING DEEPER

*Never lose an opportunity of seeing anything that is
beautiful; for beauty is God's handwriting—a wayside
sacrament. Welcome it in every fair face, in
every fair sky, in every fair flower, and thank
God for it as a cup of blessing.*

RALPH WALDO EMERSON

No matter where we are on life's seas—in the doldrums,
in a hurricane, or in calm waters—we all need wind in our
sails to move forward. But what exactly is that wind, that
breath of fresh air, that energy-giving force that draws you
in and inspires you? How do we find that intangible, life-
giving X factor that fuels personal passion?

The X factor is actually inside us. It's something we
experience, something we breathe in so that we can then
breathe life wherever we're planted. Life-giving people and
churches make an enormous impact in subtle ways. Their
enthusiasm, positive approach, and energy for loving other
people breathe life into those around them and transform
the entire environment.

If you're serious about catching this refreshing breeze of
God, then you have to keep your love for God alive. Here's

the real secret: you can fulfill the commands of the Bible better by falling in love with God than you can by trying to obey him. It's not that obedience isn't significant or relevant; it's simply not the center of the wheel. The hub of our lives must be relationship with God. Our behavior and obedience radiate like spokes from the center of our lives and allow us to roll forward. When we try to put external behavior at the center of our wheel, we get stuck. Forward motion must be fueled by love.

To learn how to enrich your home, church, or workplace with the key elements of a life-giving culture, read chapters 2 and 3 in *Fresh Air*.

1. *Would you say the "seeds" the Lord has planted in your life are thriving and multiplying? Why or why not?*

2. *How do you feel God has uniquely designed you, and how can you use those gifts to serve others?*

3. How can we choose today to make the needs of others our primary focus?

4. What changes need to be made in order to cultivate life-giving relationships in your own life?

5. All of heaven will be about our relationship with God, not our religion. What does it look like for you to have a relationship with God without the performance trap of religion?

EYES ON THE ETERNAL

BASED ON CHAPTER 4 OF *FRESH AIR*

To see a world in a grain of sand,
And a heaven in a wild flower,
Hold infinity in the palm of your hand,
And eternity in an hour.

WILLIAM BLAKE

RECAP
....

The power to live a life less ordinary, a life of purpose and impact, lies within our daily choices.

JUST FOR FUN
....

What is your most valuable possession? What makes it so valuable?

BIG IDEA

God calls us to travel light by keeping our destination in sight. When we live for eternity, our difficulties don't disappear—but they don't weigh us down, either. We can choose to focus on our problems, or we can focus on eternal things and enjoy the fresh breeze of joyful purpose. Live for eternity, and you'll never live another day unfulfilled.

VIEW

Watch the DVD session by Pastor Chris Hodges entitled "Eyes on the Eternal." Think about the following:

In which area or areas of your life are you feeling unfulfilled?

Can you name your primary focus?

How can you focus more on eternity?

LEARNING TO BREATHE

....

Since, then, you have been raised with Christ, set your hearts on things above, where Christ is, seated at the right hand of God. Set your minds on things above, not on earthly things.

COLOSSIANS 3:1-2

1. *Make a list of the things that are the most important to you.*

2. *What is your reason for being on the planet?*

3. *In* Fresh Air, *Pastor Chris compares the perspectives of two biblical greats, Solomon and Paul. (See pages 53 through 56.) How did their focus affect the impact they made on God's people? What are you currently doing that will have an eternal impact?*

PRAY

....

Pray for group members to connect with their purpose and discover practical ways to move toward it.

NOTES

GOING DEEPER

Aim at heaven and you get earth thrown in.
Aim at earth and you get neither.

C. S. LEWIS

Many times things don't work out the way we had hoped
. . . and there's nothing like unfulfilled expectations to take
the wind out of our sails. But what we see and experience
around us is not all there is. If we want to enjoy life in a
vibrant, fully alive way, we must choose to focus on God
and his purposes. Then we will have the strength to meet
problems big and small.

The only way to get through the really consuming problems is to fix our eyes on something beyond the pain. Take,
for example, a little boy who is sobbing over a scraped knee.
Yet when his mom pulls a Popsicle from the fridge—presto,
the tears disappear and a smile starts to form. Granted, we
often face things far more consuming than a hurt knee, but
the point remains: there is more to life than our present
circumstances, and how we deal with our situation has everything to do with where we choose to focus our attention.

Paul encouraged us to take a different position from the
one most of us usually choose. "Since, then, you have been
raised with Christ, set your hearts on things above, where

Christ is, seated at the right hand of God. Set your minds on things above, not on earthly things" (Colossians 3:1-2).

What are you looking at when you think about where you are in your life right now? Could it be that your problems are not the real problem? Maybe you just have the wrong focus. Maybe you're expecting from the world what can only come from God. Or are you expecting to receive from others what God alone can give?

For specific activities that can restore our spirits and help us invest in eternity, read chapter 4 in the book *Fresh Air*.

1. *How have your unmet expectations taken the wind out of your sails? Is there anything in your life that is undermining your contentment or stealing your hope?*

2. *The secret to living life with wind in your sails is to focus on more than your problems and pain. What are your eyes fixed on? What changes do you need to make to focus on what really matters? What do you need to spend less time doing?*

3. *How has God moved on your behalf this week? If nothing comes to mind, ask him to reveal the ways he has shown his love to you this week.*

ATTITUDE ADJUSTMENT

BASED ON CHAPTER 5 OF *FRESH AIR*

Everything can be taken from a man [or a woman] but one thing: the last of the human freedoms—to choose one's attitude in any given set of circumstances, to choose one's own way.

VIKTOR FRANKL, in writing about his experience in concentration camps

RECAP

When we focus on the promises of heaven, problems on earth become less important and less burdensome. When we focus on the needs of others, we gain a new perspective on our own problems.

JUST FOR FUN

Who in your life do you love spending time with? Describe their attitude.

BIG IDEA

Attitude is a choice. Fortunately, attitudes can be adjusted. It starts by taking responsibility for your own attitude and learning from others who model fresh-air attributes. We need to allow the Spirit of God to transform us from the inside out because we can't always determine what happens *to* us, but we can determine what happens *in* us.

VIEW

Watch the DVD session by Pastor Chris Hodges entitled "Attitude Adjustment." Think about the following:

What are some fresh-air qualities?

Which of these qualities are reflected in you?

What determines your attitude?

CATCH YOUR BREATH

People who have God's breath on the inside seem to

- savor each day as a gift;
- draw others to themselves;

- relish each new day as one of promise, hope, opportunity, and optimism;
- rarely complain or dwell on losses;
- remember the past without being tied to it;
- enjoy the present;
- anticipate the future; and
- gave influence and use it to encourage and shape others.

LEARNING TO BREATHE

Let the Spirit renew your thoughts and attitudes. . . . Imitate God, therefore, in everything you do, because you are his dear children. Live a life filled with love, following the example of Christ.
EPHESIANS 4:23; 5:1-2, NLT

1. *This week you met Billy Hornsby, whom Pastor Chris describes as the most life-giving person he's ever met. He says Billy "gave us a glimpse into what Jesus is like." Read pages 70 through 75 in* Fresh Air; *then describe what Scripture tells us about how Christ imparted life, love, joy, and peace to those around him.*

2. *Who has modeled a great attitude for you, and how have they influenced you to grow closer to God and be a life-giver?*

3. *Read Philippians 2:5-8 and list the attitudes of Jesus.*

4. *If you truly want to live life to the fullest—to have real joy, peace, purpose, and satisfaction—then find a way to make these truths your own and become part of who you really are. Take a minute to ask Jesus what he wants to speak to you about your attitude. Write down what he says to you.*

PRAY

Pray for group members to be filled with grace and love from the Father and for the attitudes of Jesus to be worked into their hearts.

NOTES

GOING DEEPER

The longer I live, the more I realize the impact of
attitude on life. . . . We cannot change our past. . . .
We cannot change the fact that people will act in a
certain way. . . . The only thing we can do is play
on the one string we have, and that is our attitude.
I am convinced that life is 10 percent what happens
to me and 90 percent how I react to it.

CHARLES SWINDOLL

People who have God's breath inside of them seem to savor each day as a gift. They enjoy life to the fullest. They smile, and they laugh! Their lives aren't any easier than anyone else's, and yet they rarely complain or dwell on their losses. They remember the past without remaining tied to it. They enjoy the present as a tremendous gift. They anticipate the future with great hope.

Perhaps those attributes sound appealing to you but also seem completely unrealistic. Well, there's good news. Jesus came to restore our relationship with God and to put fresh air back in our lives. One reason people loved being around Jesus was that he gave the people around him life, energy, peace, and joy. When we don't believe this, we tend to define our faith, or more accurately, our religion, as a series of dos and don'ts. Jesus addressed our joyless living when he said, "The thief's purpose is to steal and kill and destroy. My purpose is to give them a rich and satisfying life" (John 10:10, NLT).

When we're pulled and pushed from one set of demands and expectations to another—home to work to school to church—always reacting and trying to survive, there never seems to be time to be proactive and get ahead. And when we just try to keep up with everyone else, we lose our joy.

But the best day of your life is today, the one you're currently in! Accept the present as the gift God intends it to be and make the most of it.

Discover specific—and surprising—ways to bring fresh air back into your attitude by reading chapter 5 in *Fresh Air*.

1. *One reason people loved being around Jesus was that he brought life, energy, peace, and joy to every situation. When we are just trying to keep up with everyone else, we lose our joy. Are you following that example in your own life?*

2. *Ask God to begin to give you a glimpse of the joy Jesus saw when he went to the cross for you. How does that affect the way you view your circumstances?*

3. *Unforgiveness is like drinking poison and expecting someone else to die. In order to enjoy life, we need to learn to forgive. Who do you need to forgive today?*

ALIVE

BASED ON CHAPTERS 6 THROUGH 9 OF *FRESH AIR*

Come, Thou Fount of every blessing,
tune my heart to sing Thy grace;
Streams of mercy, never ceasing,
call for songs of loudest praise.
Teach me some melodious sonnet,
sung by flaming tongues above.
Praise the mount, I'm fixed upon it,
mount of Thy redeeming love.

ROBERT ROBINSON
"Come, Thou Fount of Every Blessing"

RECAP

To gain a proper perspective on life, we must adjust our attitudes—no longer being conformed to the pattern of this world, but rather being transformed by the renewing of our minds through the Word of God (Romans 12:2).

JUST FOR FUN

If safety or money were not an issue, what is the most daring thing you would try?

BIG IDEA

If you want to be alive with fresh air, meditate on the Word; settle on its authority; practice a real prayer life; know God's love language; and build healthy relationships.

VIEW

Watch the DVD session by Pastor Chris Hodges entitled "Alive." Think about the following:

We are made up of three parts (see 1 Thessalonians 5:23). What are they, and which of these three should be in charge?

What are four things that can help you switch from a life of duty to one of devotion?

CATCH YOUR BREATH

Most of the time, we think about whatever we worship.

- What do you think about the most?
- What are you thinking about right now?
- Who or what is the object of your affection?

LEARNING TO BREATHE

1. *Can you think of a time when you had a revelation from the Word of God, something that spoke specifically to you and your situation? What was it, and how did it help you? In what area of your life do you need a revelation?*

2. *Read Matthew 6:9-13. Take five minutes, and using the Lord's Prayer as an outline, write a prayer from your heart.*

3. *In* The Five Love Languages, *author Gary Chapman uses the term* love language *to describe the ways we like to receive love. Those five ways are quality time, acts of service, physical touch, words of affirmation, and gift giving. Share with the group what you think your primary love language is.*

4. *The Bible tells us God's love language is praise (consider the book of Psalms). Look back at pages 118 through 122 in* Fresh Air *to review the seven types of praise that God loves to receive from us. How have you praised God in the past? What other ways are there to praise God? Challenge one another to try something new this week.*

PRAY

Pray for group members to receive a revelation from God's Word. Ask him to teach them how to pray and worship in spirit and truth (John 4:23-24).

NOTES

GOING DEEPER

Turn around and believe that the good news that
we are loved is better than we ever dared hope, and
that to believe in that good news, to live out of it and
toward it, to be in love with that good news, is of all
glad things in this world the gladdest thing of all.

FREDERICK BUECHNER

How would you describe your relationship with your Bible right now? Do you feel a twinge of guilt when the topic comes up because you feel like you should read it more often or more closely? When you are indifferent about God's Word, it keeps you stranded in the doldrums.

The Bible is far more than an ancient manual; it is a divine wind machine, giving us direction and purpose. Jesus said, "The Spirit gives life; the flesh counts for nothing. The words I have spoken to you—they are full of the Spirit [breath] and life" (John 6:63). In the original Greek language, in which the New Testament was written, the word *spirit* literally means "breath."

Jesus is telling us that his words, the messages he came to deliver, are not normal words. Basically, he is saying, "These words I've spoken to you are breath, a blast of wind to give you life." Or, put another way, "My words are fresh air for you."

God's Word is alive and dynamic and meets you where you are. If you take it into your heart and mind, it will transform the way you live and help you discern what's from God and what's not. There's nothing too difficult, too painful, too embarrassing, too human, or too earthy for it to address. The people populating its pages can inspire you, coach you, challenge you, instruct you, and sometimes amaze you if you'll let them.

To learn how to engage more fully with God through Scripture, prayer, worship, and community, read chapters 6 through 9 in the book *Fresh Air*.

1. *Prayer is simply communication with God, and when we talk with him, we are changed from the inside out. Are you experiencing the blessing of an active prayer life?*

2. *The Bible is far more than an ancient manual; it is a divine wind machine that gives us direction and purpose. How can you activate the power of the Word in your life?*

3. *God wants you to live a full life, free of the baggage of past pain, hurt, and disappointments. Ask him to reveal the places where you need his healing, and choose to exchange the past for the new, good things he has for you. Write down what he says to you here.*

MONEY MATTERS

BASED ON CHAPTER 10 OF *FRESH AIR*

*You must gain control over your money or
the lack of it will forever control you.*

DAVE RAMSEY

RECAP

There is more to life than obligation and duty. Knowing God's Word and discovering ways to know him better make it possible to live a truly authentic and joyful life.

JUST FOR FUN

If you were given $100 to spend for a day, what would you do with it?

BIG IDEA

In order to experience a breath of fresh air in your finances, you must cultivate an attitude of contentment and maintain practices that give life.

VIEW

Watch the DVD session by Pastor Chris Hodges entitled "Money Matters." Think about the following:

Are you on financial life support?   YES   NO

What are four values and three complementary practices that can move you out of the financial doldrums?

Why are finances important to God?

What is margin, and why is it important?

CATCH YOUR BREATH

Take an honest inventory of your personal finances.

- Would you be willing to publicly disclose your finances without fear of impropriety?

- Do you look for ways to give to others?
- Can God trust you to share your resources regularly?
- When you make money decisions, do you have an eternal mind-set?

LEARNING TO BREATHE

1. *Money is a part of our everyday lives. Why then do so many of us struggle to manage our finances well?*

2. *Often we become blinded by our desire to have it all right now, no matter what, which steals from our future. How has the myth of more affected you? What principles could help alleviate that pressure?*

3. *Read pages 151 through 153 of* Fresh Air, *paying particular attention to Luke 16:10-11. Who has modeled financial integrity for you? What does it take to be a trustworthy steward?*

4. *Many of us misunderstand tithing. If tithing became more about your heart than an amount of money, how would it change your practices?*

5. *Read Haggai 1:5-6. What one thing could you change today about how you relate to your money?*

PRAY

Ask God to show group members one thing to change in the way they relate to money. Pray for the development of an eternal mind-set, a heart of generosity, and a desire to be a faithful manager of God's resources.

NOTES

GOING DEEPER

Money never made a man happy yet, nor will it.
The more a man has, the more he wants.
Instead of filling a vacuum, it makes one.
BENJAMIN FRANKLIN

Perhaps nothing can cut a river of fear and anxiety through our lives more than financial troubles. So many of us are on financial life support, barely making ends meet and holding our breath every month to see if we have enough to pay the bills and meet our expenses. We're gasping for air and laboring over each breath.

> *Give careful thought to your ways. You have planted much, but harvested little. You eat, but never have enough. You drink, but never have your fill. You put on clothes, but are not warm. You earn wages, only to put them in a purse with holes in it. (Haggai 1:5-6)*

Yet God's heart is that of a giver—for God so loved the world that he gave (John 3:16). The Word tells us that he withholds no good thing from his people (Psalm 84:11). He is the God of more than enough, not barely enough.

It is natural for us to model generosity as the people of God. And it's not just money. God's people are supposed

43

to be conduits of his extravagant love and abundant provision. We must cultivate an attitude of contentment and maintain practices that give life and values based on God's Word in order to move out of the fury of the financial storm and into calm waters.

Financial integrity is a breath of fresh air, and God's principles are the bedrock of that integrity. When we develop wise principles and live abundantly generous lives, we will be modeling the character of God.

> *As it is written: "They have freely scattered their gifts to the poor; their righteousness endures forever." Now he who supplies seed to the sower and bread for food will also supply and increase your store of seed and will enlarge the harvest of your righteousness. You will be enriched in every way so that you can be generous on every occasion, and through us your generosity will result in thanksgiving to God. (2 Corinthians 9:9-11)*

For guiding principles that will help you experience a breath of fresh air in your finances, read chapter 10 in *Fresh Air*.

1. *The Bible says we are blessed to bless others. How can you bless someone today?*

2. *In order to experience a breath of fresh air in our finances, it's time for a new way of thinking. What steps can we take to move out of the fury of a financial storm and into calm waters?*

3. *The bottom line of any accounts ledger should be on eternity; we must live to give. Take a look at your past month's finances. Do they reflect Kingdom purpose? Write down what God is saying to you.*

4. *What is it that your heart longs to have? What is the objective of your life, and how does money factor into it?*

ROOM TO REST

BASED ON CHAPTER 11 OF *FRESH AIR*

Thou hast made us for thyself, O Lord, and
our heart is restless until it finds its rest in thee.

AUGUSTINE

RECAP

A breath of fresh air in finances begins with values and principles. When you practice biblical truths, you can live by principle instead of pressure.

JUST FOR FUN

Describe your ideal restful day. Where would you be and what would you do? Who would you want with you?

BIG IDEA

We all need a life routine that includes rest. Though culture is in direct conflict with this idea, God commands us to set aside time for renewal and relaxation because he loves us (Mark 2:27).

VIEW

Watch the DVD session by Pastor Chris Hodges entitled "Room to Rest." Think about the following:

What is the principle of the Sabbath?

Has "busy" become who you are more than what you do?

CATCH YOUR BREATH

Rest is essential to health. Become aware of things that violate your rest.

- Does your schedule include a firm space for rest?
- Are you relying on substitute solutions for rest?
- Do you feel forced by habit into fulfilling the urgent agendas of everyone else?

LEARNING TO BREATHE

1. *We have personal indicators, much like the warning light on a car's dashboard, that tell us we need to rest. Name some things that signal your need for rest.*

2. *Jesus warned us against being stretched past our limits. In what areas of your life do you feel stretched past your limit?*

3. *Review the four strategies for beginning to incorporate the Sabbath rest into your life on pages 176 through 177 of* Fresh Air. *How might these help you to develop a plan in your life for rest—daily, weekly, monthly, and annually? Discuss Sabbath principles and practical ways to apply them to your life.*

4. *Read Psalm 90:12. Now, take a few moments privately to ask God what needs to change in order for you to practice Sabbath in your life. Record what he shows you.*

PRAY
. . . .

Ask the Lord to show group members the truth about rest.

NOTES
. . . .

GOING DEEPER

My yoke is easy and my burden is light.

JESUS CHRIST, Matthew 11:30

We may be in the doldrums and have no breath of life filling our sails because we never stop our ship to rest and recalibrate ourselves. Did you know that God created a principle to keep us from burning out or breaking down emotionally, physically, and spiritually? That principle is called the Sabbath, and it's all about rest and renewal.

To understand this day of rest, we need to understand the concept behind it. The Sabbath principle demonstrates that by honoring God's design, we can get more done with less. It's not a law requiring us to honor the seventh day, as some people might think. It's a truth about how we're made and what we really need.

When we are ignoring the principle of Sabbath rest, no vacation will soothe the depths of our exhaustion. Instead, we need a comprehensive life routine that includes rest as a key component. We need to make some type of commitment—daily, weekly, monthly, and annually—to intentionally and deliberately rest. If this sounds like a pipe dream to you, stop right now and ask the Lord to open the eyes of your heart to hear the truth about rest.

When we are rested and refreshed, we are better able to think straight and with a long-term perspective. We have clarity about our priorities and what we're actually committed to in our lives. Real rest comes when our minds are relaxed because we know that God is in charge. It's a matter of trust.

For tips on how to experience "Sabbath rest" and discover true refreshment in life, read chapter 11 in *Fresh Air*.

1. *We can't function without rest; it's simply how we're made. Ask the Lord to open the eyes of your heart to hear the truth about developing specific times for rest in your own life.*

2. *We are more productive when we regularly include rest in our schedules than when we continue to push ourselves. Ask the Holy Spirit to reveal ways you can arrange your schedule to incorporate the rest and refreshment God desires for you.*

3. *If you want to experience a breath of fresh air in your life, then you have to resist the temptation to keep going at the same pace all of the time. What would it look like for you to have a weekly Sabbath rest?*

4. *Real rest comes when our minds relax because we know God is in charge. What does real rest look like in your life?*

THE SOURCE OF BREATH

BASED ON CHAPTERS 12 AND 13 OF *FRESH AIR*

This is the tragedy and woe of the hour—that we neglect the most important One who could possibly be in our midst—the Holy Spirit of God. Then, in order to make up for His absence, we have to do something to keep up our own spirits.

A. W. TOZER

RECAP

We need a comprehensive life routine that includes rest as a key component.

JUST FOR FUN

If you could spend fifteen minutes with any living person, who would it be and why?

BIG IDEA

If you want a breath of fresh air, you need to have a vibrant relationship with the Holy Spirit. He is a continuous power source, a best friend, a trail guide, and a direct link to God himself.

VIEW

Watch the DVD session by Pastor Chris Hodges entitled "The Source of Breath." Think about the following:

What are some of your preconceived notions about the Holy Spirit?

Who is the Holy Spirit?

What are some of the benefits of the Holy Spirit?

LEARNING TO BREATHE

1. *What is the first thing that comes to your mind when you hear the name "Holy Spirit"?*

2. *When and where did you first learn about the Holy Spirit?*

3. *How would you describe your current relationship with the Holy Spirit?*

4. *Read John 14:17, John 16:7, along with pages 196 through 198 of* Fresh Air. *Sort through your ideas and feelings connected to the Holy Spirit. Are your beliefs about the Holy Spirit based on God's Word?*

5. *Read John 3:8. The wind, though unseen, is identified by its activity and effects, and the same is true of the Holy Spirit. Mystery is a part of our relationship with the Holy Spirit. What are your thoughts about that?*

6. *Read John 16:13-15. In what area of your life do you need guidance from God? Remember, the Holy Spirit is God, the Counselor, the ultimate breath of fresh air.*

PRAY

Ask God to reveal who the Holy Spirit really is and to show group members the importance of his role in their lives.

NOTES

GOING DEEPER

To fall in love with God is the greatest of all romances;
to seek him, the greatest adventure; to find him,
the greatest human achievement.

AUGUSTINE

God never intended for us to make life work through our own efforts. He has provided us with a continuous power source, best friend, trail guide, and direct link to him.

At the center of it all is this: God longs to be intimately involved with our lives. This is the very reason he sent his Son to earth to live as a man and defeat death for all time. With this victory, Jesus gave us a gift, an ongoing breath of fresh air in our lives. The source of that blast of life-breath in us is the Holy Spirit of God.

Consider this: Trying to live the Christian life without the power of the Holy Spirit is like getting the keys to a brand-new car without any gas in the tank. Often we have a belief system but no power or desire to carry out the truths of Scripture. We exist as weak believers for fear of what our lives might look like if we surrendered to God 100 percent. Somehow it seems safer to have just enough of God to get to heaven, but not so much that he radically alters our lives.

Knowing the Holy Spirit as a friend changes everything for the better. The Holy Spirit is our lifeline to the Father; he's the one who empowers us to become who we were created to be. If you haven't already, open your heart to the Word and find out for yourself what the Spirit is really all about.

- The Holy Spirit is God (Acts 5:3-4)
- The Holy Spirit is the lifeline to the Father (John 16:7)
- The Holy Spirit is the author of the Bible (John 6:63; 2 Timothy 3:16-17)
- The Holy Spirit is our counselor and teacher (John 14:16-17, 26)
- The Holy Spirit is our guide in relationships (Psalm 43:3; Psalm 48:14; Isaiah 58:11)

To find out more about how the Holy Spirit makes relationship with God a grand adventure, read chapters 12 and 13 in *Fresh Air*.

1. *We are spiritual beings having temporary physical experiences on earth. How does this affect your perspective on the problems of your life?*

2. The word Spirit *in Scripture means "breath." How have you seen the breath of God move in your own life?*

3. *God's ways are not our ways and his thoughts are not our thoughts (see Isaiah 55:8). In order to receive all he has for us, we have to get comfortable with the unexpected and unpredictable. Has the Holy Spirit ever spoken to you in a way you didn't expect?*

4. *The Holy Spirit is a person who wants to relate to us personally. He is more than we could hope for or imagine, our lifeline to the Father, and a better Encourager and Comforter than we have ever known. How has he shown one of his attributes to you?*

5. *We need the Holy Spirit as our friend every day: to remain connected to God, to talk to him, to feel his presence, and to experience his power. How can you connect with the Holy Spirit today?*

6. *You'll find the best in any relationship when you put your whole heart into it. When you take a leap of faith to fully commit to God, you will find the greatest spiritual adventure you have ever known. Picture yourself going deeper in your relationship with God, and write down what you look forward to experiencing with him.*

NEXT STEPS

BASED ON CHAPTER 14 OF *FRESH AIR*

Never be afraid to trust an
unknown future to a known God.

CORRIE TEN BOOM

RECAP

The Holy Spirit is vital to our relationship with God. He empowers us to become who we were created to be and points us to truth. If we embrace him and access his power, we will experience revival, healing, and reconciliation.

JUST FOR FUN

What has been your favorite part of this group?

BIG IDEA

Life with God is a great adventure, filled with intimate friendship with the Holy Spirit. Just like any important relationship, we must invest ourselves in order to see it grow and thrive.

VIEW

Watch the DVD session by Pastor Chris Hodges entitled "Next Steps." Think about the following:

What practical things can you do to grow your relationship with the Holy Spirit?

How can you maintain healthy relationships (Ecclesiastes 4:12)?

LEARNING TO BREATHE

1. *Read Revelation 12:11. Testify—which means tell—about what God has done in you through this study.*

2. How can you be a refreshing source to the people around you?

3. How can you avoid going back into the doldrums?

4. What will it take to maintain what we have experienced together?

5. The Holy Spirit makes life with God an adventure. Just for fun, create your own bucket list—those things you've always dreamed of doing before you "kick the bucket." This may seem like an odd exercise, but creating a bucket list can be fun, and it stirs in us a driving passion to live a richer life—one full of the breath of God. So go ahead, dream with God again and reignite the passions he put inside you.

PRAY

Pray for group members to experience the "amazing grace of the Master, Jesus Christ, the extravagant love of God, [and] the intimate friendship of the Holy Spirit" (2 Corinthians 13:14, *The Message*).

NOTES

LEADER'S GUIDE

....

Thank you for having the courage to shepherd others in a small group! Being a servant leader brings unique blessings, and leading a small group is a trust and a privilege. Before the group launches and before each weekly meeting, set aside time with God and ask him to fill you and touch you with his passion, his purity, and the power of his Holy Spirit. To be an effective leader, you have to be in an intimate relationship with Jesus: full of his love and the Holy Spirit. In other words, to share him, you have to know him. To fulfill his purposes for your group, you have to know what those purposes are.

GET STARTED

Invite the Holy Spirit to be a part of the group from the very start. Before each session, we encourage you to pray, preview the material and DVD, and prepare your own heart to be real with your group. And you do not have to teach! Rely on the DVDs to help participants learn the principles. The goal isn't to go through all of the material but to build relationships in your group. Your job as a leader is not to have all of the answers, but to move each member one step closer to God and others in authentic relationship.

PRAYER WORKS

Make a commitment to pray for your participants by name outside of group time. Then watch God move in their lives! Enlist the help of your co-leader or a trusted friend and agree together in prayer for your group's needs and shared concerns. Pray for the Lord to open eyes and hearts and to touch each member of your group in a unique way. "The prayer of a righteous person is powerful and effective" (James 5:16).

PREVIEW, PLEASE

It is most helpful to watch the session before you facilitate it. You will notice key points and have the opportunity to ask the Lord for insight and direction. Walking through the study in advance will help you anticipate discussion topics and get comfortable with the flow of the session.

MINISTRY MOVES

Fight the battles in your group spiritually through prayer, and leave the heavy lifting to God. When you minister to individuals, simply encourage them, share Scripture, and pray. Proverbs 27:23 tells us, "Be sure you know the condition of your flocks, give careful attention to your herds." Your primary role as a small group leader is to know where people are spiritually and to help move them a step closer to Christ during the study. For example, if they need to understand the gospel message, bring them to a service where they can hear it clearly presented. If they haven't been baptized, let them know about a baptism service.

STAY FREE

It is not your responsibility to create spiritual growth in your participants' lives. That is the job of the Holy Spirit. For starters, get to know the members of your group. How did they come to know Christ? Or do they know Christ? Who has been an influence in their lives? What are their biggest dreams? Care about their hearts. Relationship enhances our ability to minister during times of need.

YOU MATTER

The power of personal testimony is real and engaging. Don't be afraid to share with your group what God is doing in your heart. Briefly share your trials and victories as appropriate. We promise that people will relate. "They triumphed over him by the blood of the Lamb and by the word of their testimony" (Revelation 12:11).

TRY TEAMWORK

Ask God to help you build a healthy leadership team. If you can enlist a co-leader to help you lead the group, you will find your experience to be much easier. Additionally, a co-leader can help you identify and equip potential new leaders. "Two are better than one, because they have a good return for their labor. If either of them falls down, one can help the other up" (Ecclesiastes 4:9-10).

BE YOURSELF

God wants you to use your unique gifts and personality. Don't try to do things exactly like another leader; do them in a way that fits you. Remember that it is common for good leaders to feel that they are not ready to lead. Moses, Solomon, Jeremiah, and Timothy were all reluctant to lead. Yet God promises, "Never will I leave you; never will I forsake you" (Hebrews 13:5).

PRACTICE PATIENCE

When you ask a question, be patient. Someone will eventually respond. Sometimes people need a moment or two of silence to think about the question. After someone answers, affirm the response with a simple "Thanks" or "Good job." Then ask, "How about somebody else?" or "Would someone who hasn't shared like to add anything?" Be sensitive to new people or reluctant members who aren't ready to say, pray, or do anything. If you give them a safe setting, they are likely to open up over time.

THINK SMALL

If your group has a large number of participants or members of both genders, consider breaking up into small circles at the end to pray or share. A small circle encourages a quiet person to participate and tends to minimize the effects of a more vocal or dominant member.

PLAN DETAILS

Make sure all members are informed of the following specifics. Be consistent and predictable, which will make members more comfortable. Taking care of details ahead of time communicates to your group that you care.

- *Be consistent in when, where, and how long you meet.* Show honor and respect for others' time and commitments by faithfully beginning and ending on time.
- *Politely handle media and minimize interruptions.* Ask members to silence cell phones, house phones, televisions, and children (just kidding) during your meeting.
- *Consider child care needs.*
- *Arrange for refreshments or meals.*

BE CREATIVE

If you feel you need a little jolt to get the group talking and laughing, try this icebreaker idea, or come up with your own. Give everyone a card and ask them to write down one fun fact about themselves that they are pretty sure no one else in the group knows. Or ask a vision question like "If you could do anything you wanted and you knew you couldn't fail, what would you do?" Collect the cards and shuffle them without looking. Read off the results and invite the group to guess who wrote the card. Let the interaction flow for a while.

LOVE LIKE JESUS

Leading people to fresh air is all about allowing Jesus' breath, life, peace, and joy to saturate your life. Once you have experienced this life-changing love, you may make the difference in other people's lives just by listening to and loving them. Remember this: God is love, and as a group leader, you are in a prime position to pass this love on to others!

NOTES

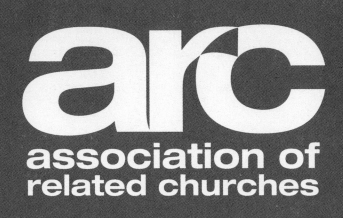

Launching and growing life-giving churches

Are you a church planter or church leader, or do you belong to a church in transition? The Association of Related Churches (ARC) offers support, guidance, and resources in four key ways:

- *We help you start strong.* We show you how to build your launch team, raise funds, form a worship team, develop your children's ministry, and gain momentum—so you can open your doors with excellence. If you start strong, you have a greater chance of growing strong.

- *We reach the unchurched.* With more than 110 million Americans never or rarely attending church, it's critical that we cross cultural walls to reach the lost. ARC is all about helping churches stay culturally relevant—characterized by Bible-based teaching, authentic relationships, and dynamic family ministries.

- *We build relationships.* Solid relationships are the foundation for growth in any aspect of life. As ARC churches multiply across the country, you'll join an ever-expanding group of people who are committed to one another's success.

- *We support financially.* We know that it takes money to do ministry. That's why ARC invests financially into the vision of starting new churches.

For more information, visit ARC online at www.weplantlife.com.